EMPEROR PENGUIN

BIRD OF THE ANTARCTIC

Jean-Claude Deguine

The Stephen Greene Press
Brattleboro, Vermont

First American Edition

This book was printed in Great Britain.
It is published by The Stephen Greene Press,
Brattleboro, Vermont 05301.

Library of Congress Catalog Card Number: 74-5224
International Standard Book Number: 0-8289-0235-6 (paper)
                                    0-8289-0236-4 (cloth)

Antarctica, one of the seven continents of the world, is a great ice-covered land mass accessible by sea only in summer, towards the end of the year. After passing a barrier of immense icebergs, the ship travels through miles of pack-ice or broken sea-ice to Antarctica, where the men unload food and scientific equipment, and everything they will need for survival until the following spring. The ship then leaves, to return a year later.

In October, the Adélie penguins arrive from further north, returning to the traditional rookeries which have been established for centuries. Men have found their sites so sheltered that they too use them for their huts. Adélie penguins build nests of small stones and breed in summer. The female lays two eggs and she and the male alternate, sharing the incubation time, tucking the eggs between their shanks so that they never come in contact with the cold ground or air. Once hatched, the chicks must soon brave the Antarctic cold and later, the threat of being preyed upon at sea by the leopard seal.

In summer, the sea-birds, the snow petrel, the cape pigeon and the skua find food in the sea which is rich with prawn and plankton. The Adélie penguins must be wary of the skua, a predatory bird, which will snatch unprotected eggs.

There are no land animals in Antarctica, only sea animals. However, seals can spend long periods on land or on floating ice although they court and mate in the water.

Seals always produce their young on land. Lazily snuggling
against its mother, a newborn Weddell seal opens its eyes
on a stretch of ice in the spring sunshine.

In March, the birds, the Adélie penguins and the seals leave for the north and a warmer climate.

Then one day across the stretch of polar ice and snow, the Emperor penguins arrive from the north where they have spent the summer eating vast quantities of food in preparation for the long winter.

Majestically they file to their meeting place between the ice cliffs. They return to the same breeding grounds year after year.

They walk for miles in stately lines until they have all gathered together, about twelve thousand Emperor penguins, each one faithfully looking for his mate of the previous year. Unless the male or female has died, each penguin returns to the same partner.

Perhaps these penguins are late. Penguins do not fly: if they have to travel many miles over the ice, they toboggan on their stomachs with their wings helping to push them forward. This way they move much more quickly.

The penguins are courting. Sometimes a male tries to befriend a female who has not yet found her partner. When the true mate does arrive, there is a dignified discussion and the intruder leaves to find his own mate.

After much parading and signalling, the penguins eventually find one another. Then they go off quietly somewhere to mate.

Meanwhile the males remain, incubating the eggs through the worst of the winter, huddled together against the blizzards and icy polar winds. The temperature can be 40 degrees below zero, but there is no chance for a male penguin to replace his weight loss: with an egg on his feet, he can walk neither far nor fast. The incubating male penguins remain almost immobilized until the females return.

The female lays her egg in late June or early July, nearly a month after arriving at the rookery. The male then takes charge of it, carrying it on his feet, under the soft, warm fold of skin. The female travels across the ice to feed in the fish-filled waters far away to the north: she must be in good condition when the chick hatches in about eight weeks time.

Almost exactly eight weeks later, the females return from
their long trek, drawn back to their mates by a curious and
amazing instinct, to relieve the male and to feed the chick.

The chicks stand naked on their parents' feet.

The long fast of the male is over: he has lost about half
his weight. While the female looks after the chick the
male makes the long journey to the open sea to satisfy
his appetite and then returns with food for the chick.
The mother, in her turn, will travel to the sea and come
back with more fish for her young.

The parents feed the chick by regurgitating fish they have eaten.

Gradually, the chick grows. Under the watchful care of its parents it will soon be able to venture from the adult's side . . .

. . . but not yet. One eager and curious chick wanders away too soon and loses its parents. It finds shelter with other adult penguins until its parents claim it.

Once the chicks are old enough, both parents can go to the sea together for food. They leave their young huddled in a nursery to keep warm and safe. A group of adults watches them. Even so, many chicks die from cold and hunger. A blizzard can start in a few minutes and the fierce lashings of snow and wind can freeze any unprotected young.

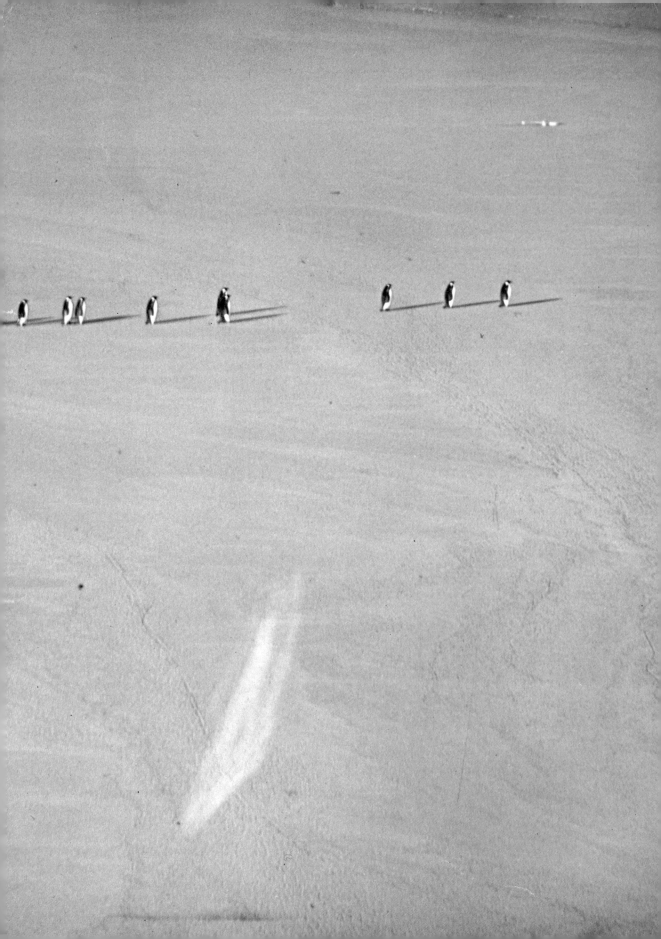

In October, at the beginning of the Antarctic summer, the penguins begin to migrate. They file across the ice from their rookery, which can be many miles from the sea, and they gather in groups at the edge of the sea-ice.

They wait for the ice to break into ice-floe rafts on which they can drift northwards. If the young are to survive, they must complete their moult before the ice-floes melt and they have to enter the water. The Emperor penguins leave, to return again next autumn. Of all the penguin species, only the Emperor breeds in the Antarctic in the harsh winter months.

Now that it is spring, the Adélie penguins, the seals and
the sea-birds migrate to the Antarctic for the summer.

Now, too, the ship can return to Antarctica

miles

0	200	400	800	1200	1600

Scale